Applying the Standards:
STEM
Grade 5

Credits
Content Editor: Mary K. Corcoran
Copy Editor: Julie B. Killian

Visit *carsondellosa.com* for correlations to Common Core, state, national, and Canadian provincial standards.

Carson-Dellosa Publishing, LLC
PO Box 35665
Greensboro, NC 27425 USA
carsondellosa.com

ISBN 978-1-4838-1576-3
02-278151151

Table of Contents

Introduction

STEM education is a growing force in today's classroom. Exposure to science, technology, engineering, and math is important in twenty-first century learning as it allows students to succeed in higher education as well as a variety of careers.

While it can come in many forms, STEM education is most often presented as an engaging task that asks students to solve a problem. Additionally, creativity, collaboration, communication, and critical thinking are integral to every task. STEM projects are authentic learning tasks that guide students to address a variety of science and math standards. Also, students strengthen English Language Arts skills by recording notes and written reflections throughout the process.

In this book, students are asked to complete a range of tasks with limited resources. Materials for each task are limited to common household objects. Students are guided through each task by the steps of the engineering design process to provide a framework through which students can grow their comfort level and independently complete tasks.

Use the included rubric to guide assessment of student responses and further plan any necessary remediation. Confidence in STEM tasks will help students succeed in their school years and beyond.

Student Roles

Student collaboration is an important component of STEM learning. Encourage collaboration by having students complete tasks in groups. Teach students to communicate openly, support each other, and respect the contributions of all members. Keep in mind that collaborative grouping across achievement levels can provide benefits for all students as they pool various perspectives and experiences toward a group goal.

Consider assigning formal roles to students in each group. This will simplify the collaborative tasks needed to get a project done and done well. The basic roles of group structure are as follows:

- The *captain* leads and guides other students in their roles.

- The *guide* walks the team through the steps, keeps track of time, and encourages the team to try again.

- The *materials manager* gathers, organizes, and guides the use of materials.

- The *reporter* records the team's thoughts and reports on the final project to the class.

STEM Performance Rubric

Use this rubric as a guide for assessing students' project management skills. It can also be offered to students as a tool to show your expectations and scoring. Note: Some items may not apply to each project.

4	_____	Asks or identifies comprehensive high-level questions
	_____	Makes valid, nontrivial inferences based on evidence in the text
	_____	Uses an appropriate, complete strategy to solve the problem
	_____	Skillfully justifies the solution and strategy used
	_____	Offers insightful reasoning and strong evidence of critical thinking
	_____	Collaborates with others in each stage of the process
	_____	Effectively evaluates and organizes information and outcomes
3	_____	Asks or identifies ample high-level questions
	_____	Exhibits effective imagination and creativity
	_____	Uses an appropriate but incomplete strategy to solve the problem
	_____	Justifies answer and strategy used
	_____	Offers sufficient reasoning and evidence of critical thinking
	_____	Collaborates with others in most stages of the process
	_____	Evaluates and organizes some information or outcomes
2	_____	Asks or identifies a few related questions
	_____	Exhibits little imagination and creativity
	_____	Uses an inappropriate or unclear strategy for solving the problem
	_____	Attempts to justify answers and strategy used
	_____	Demonstrates some evidence of critical thinking
	_____	Collaborates with others if prompted
	_____	Can evaluate and organize simple information and outcomes
1	_____	Is unable to ask or identify pertinent questions
	_____	Does not exhibit adequate imagination and creativity
	_____	Uses no strategy or plan for solving the problem
	_____	Does not or cannot justify answer or strategy used
	_____	Demonstrates limited or no evidence of critical thinking
	_____	Does not collaborate with others
	_____	Cannot evaluate or organize information or outcomes

 © Carson-Dellosa · CD-104856 · Applying the Standards: STEM

Name _____

Read the task. Then, follow the steps to complete the task.

How Egg-citing!

Create a "nest" into which you will drop a hard-boiled egg from different heights, trying not to crack it.

Materials

2 hard-boiled eggs	5 paper towels
string	clay
straws	pencils

Ask

What do you already know? What do you need to know to get started? Where can you find the information you need?

_____

_____

_____

Imagine

What are the possibilities? Come up with several different options.

_____

_____

_____

Plan

Choose an idea. Draw a model and label it. Consider making different models for each stage of construction or separate diagrams of more complex parts.

📓 Plan

What are your steps? Use your drawing to guide your plan. Number your steps and write clearly so others can understand them.

_____

_____

_____

_____

🛠️ Create

Follow your plan to create your model. What worked? What didn't? What did you need to change as you went through your plan? Why?

_____

_____

_____

🔄 Improve

How could you improve your model? Do you need to start over, or can you redo a single part? If it works, can it work even better?

_____

_____

_____

💬 Communicate

How well did it work? Is the problem solved? Write a statement to describe how your model meets the guidelines of the task and why it is successful.

_____

_____

_____

☀️ Reflect

What types of nests were the most successful? Why?

_____

_____

_____

_____

Name _____

Read the task. Then, follow the steps to complete the task.

That's Tree-mendous: Plant Structures

Create "tree roots" that have the ability to stabilize a "tree" in soil. Use your pencil as the tree trunk.

Materials

pencil   soil
chenille stems

Ask

What do you already know? What do you need to know to get started? Where can you find the information you need?

_____

_____

_____

Imagine

What are the possibilities? Come up with several different options.

_____

_____

_____

Plan

Choose an idea. Draw a model and label it. Consider making different models for each stage of construction or separate diagrams of more complex parts.

📝 Plan

What are your steps? Use your drawing to guide your plan. Number your steps and write clearly so others can understand them.

_____

_____

_____

_____

✂️ Create

Follow your plan to create your model. What worked? What didn't? What did you need to change as you went through your plan? Why?

_____

_____

_____

🔄 Improve

How could you improve your model? Do you need to start over, or can you redo a single part? If it works, can it work even better?

_____

_____

_____

💬 Communicate

How well did it work? Is the problem solved? Write a statement to describe how your model meets the guidelines of the task and why it is successful.

_____

_____

_____

☀️ Reflect

How did your knowledge of plant roots help you?

_____

_____

_____

_____

Name _____

Read the task. Then, follow the steps to complete the task.

Team Marble: Friction

Create a luge for marbles. Find a surface that lets the marbles go fastest.

Materials

paper towel roll, cut in half lengthwise	a variety of surfaces, such as cardboard, cloth, sand, and soil
marbles	
glue	stopwatch

Ask

What do you already know? What do you need to know to get started? Where can you find the information you need?

_____

_____

_____

Imagine

What are the possibilities? Come up with several different options.

_____

_____

_____

Plan

Choose an idea. Draw a model and label it. Consider making different models for each stage of construction or separate diagrams of more complex parts.

📓 Plan

What are your steps? Use your drawing to guide your plan. Number your steps and write clearly so others can understand them.

_____

_____

_____

_____

🔧 Create

Follow your plan to create your model. What worked? What didn't? What did you need to change as you went through your plan? Why?

_____

_____

_____

🔄 Improve

How could you improve your model? Do you need to start over, or can you redo a single part? If it works, can it work even better?

_____

_____

_____

💬 Communicate

How well did it work? Is the problem solved? Write a statement to describe how your model meets the guidelines of the task and why it is successful.

_____

_____

_____

☀️ Reflect

How does your experience of having walked on different surfaces help you explain the results of this project?

_____

_____

_____

_____

Name _____

Read the task. Then, follow the steps to complete the task.

In the Wind

Create a wind chime that can be heard from about 6 feet (2 m) away.

Materials

paper towel roll   a variety of buttons
scissors   tabletop fan
string or thread   keys (optional)
tape

🎗 Ask

What do you already know? What do you need to know to get started? Where can you find the information you need?

_____

_____

_____

💭 Imagine

What are the possibilities? Come up with several different options.

_____

_____

_____

📝 Plan

Choose an idea. Draw a model and label it. Consider making different models for each stage of construction or separate diagrams of more complex parts.

Plan

What are your steps? Use your drawing to guide your plan. Number your steps and write clearly so others can understand them.

_____

_____

_____

_____

Create

Follow your plan to create your model. What worked? What didn't? What did you need to change as you went through your plan? Why?

_____

_____

_____

Improve

How could you improve your model? Do you need to start over, or can you redo a single part? If it works, can it work even better?

_____

_____

_____

Communicate

How well did it work? Is the problem solved? Write a statement to describe how your model meets the guidelines of the task and why it is successful.

_____

_____

_____

Reflect

How did your design determine how much wind would be needed to cause a sound that could be heard from 6 feet (2 m) away?

_____

_____

_____

_____

Name _____

Read the task. Then, follow the steps to complete the task.

A Stone Wall

Create a stone wall that is strong enough to support two 1-liter bottles of water.

Materials

clay   2 1-liter bottles of water
10 medium-sized rocks

Ask

What do you already know? What do you need to know to get started? Where can you find the information you need?

_____

_____

_____

Imagine

What are the possibilities? Come up with several different options.

_____

_____

_____

Plan

Choose an idea. Draw a model and label it. Consider making different models for each stage of construction or separate diagrams of more complex parts.

Plan

What are your steps? Use your drawing to guide your plan. Number your steps and write clearly so others can understand them.

_____

_____

_____

Create

Follow your plan to create your model. What worked? What didn't? What did you need to change as you went through your plan? Why?

_____

_____

_____

Improve

How could you improve your model? Do you need to start over, or can you redo a single part? If it works, can it work even better?

_____

_____

_____

Communicate

How well did it work? Is the problem solved? Write a statement to describe how your model meets the guidelines of the task and why it is successful.

_____

_____

_____

Reflect

How did your stone wall support the bottles' weight?

_____

_____

_____

_____

Name _____

Read the task. Then, follow the steps to complete the task.

Card Trick: Magnetism

Create a house of cards without directly touching the cards during construction.

Materials

6 playing cards	tape
craft sticks	magnets
paper clips	

Caution: Keep small magnets away from young children who might mistakenly or intentionally swallow them. Seek immediate medical attention if you suspect a child may have swallowed a magnet.

Ask

What do you already know? What do you need to know to get started? Where can you find the information you need?

_____

_____

_____

Imagine

What are the possibilities? Come up with several different options.

_____

_____

_____

Plan

Choose an idea. Draw a model and label it. Consider making different models for each stage of construction or separate diagrams of more complex parts.

Plan

What are your steps? Use your drawing to guide your plan. Number your steps and write clearly so others can understand them.

_____

_____

_____

_____

Create

Follow your plan to create your model. What worked? What didn't? What did you need to change as you went through your plan? Why?

_____

_____

_____

Improve

How could you improve your model? Do you need to start over, or can you redo a single part? If it works, can it work even better?

_____

_____

_____

Communicate

How well did it work? Is the problem solved? Write a statement to describe how your model meets the guidelines of the task and why it is successful.

_____

_____

_____

Reflect

How did your placement of the paper clips help while you constructed your house of cards?

_____

_____

_____

_____

Name _____

Read the task. Then, follow the steps to complete the task.

Energy at Play

A Newton's cradle is a set of suspended spheres that show transfer of motion. Create a Newton's cradle.

Materials

shoe box
string, thread, or fishing
   line
masking tape

5 marshmallows
5 chenille stems or paper
   clips

Caution: Some methods of cutting holes in cardboard can cause injury if not done with care. This should only be done with the use of goggles and with adult supervision.

Ask

What do you already know? What do you need to know to get started? Where can you find the information you need?

_____

_____

_____

Imagine

What are the possibilities? Come up with several different options.

_____

_____

_____

Plan

Choose an idea. Draw a model and label it. Consider making different models for each stage of construction or separate diagrams of more complex parts.

📝 Plan

What are your steps? Use your drawing to guide your plan. Number your steps and write clearly so others can understand them.

_____

_____

_____

_____

🔧 Create

Follow your plan to create your model. What worked? What didn't? What did you need to change as you went through your plan? Why?

_____

_____

_____

🔄 Improve

How could you improve your model? Do you need to start over, or can you redo a single part? If it works, can it work even better?

_____

_____

_____

💬 Communicate

How well did it work? Is the problem solved? Write a statement to describe how your model meets the guidelines of the task and why it is successful.

_____

_____

_____

☀️ Reflect

How did your placement of holes in the box affect how the cradle worked?

_____

_____

_____

_____

Name _____

Read the task. Then, follow the steps to complete the task.

What's on Your Roof?

Create two buildings—one with an eco-friendly roof and one with an ordinary roof. Compare the temperatures of the buildings' interiors over time.

Materials

2 identical boxes	water
plastic bags	aluminum foil
soil	sandpaper
a variety of small plants,	craft sticks
such as moss, grasses,	newspaper
and herbs	2 thermometers

Caution: Before beginning any nature activity, ask families' permission and inquire about students' plant and animal allergies.

Ask

What do you already know? What do you need to know to get started? Where can you find the information you need?

_____

_____

_____

Imagine

What are the possibilities? Come up with several different options.

_____

_____

_____

Plan

Choose an idea. Draw a model and label it. Consider making different models for each stage of construction or separate diagrams of more complex parts.

📝 Plan

What are your steps? Use your drawing to guide your plan. Number your steps and write clearly so others can understand them.

_____

_____

_____

🔧 Create

Follow your plan to create your model. What worked? What didn't? What did you need to change as you went through your plan? Why?

_____

_____

_____

🔄 Improve

How could you improve your model? Do you need to start over, or can you redo a single part? If it works, can it work even better?

_____

_____

_____

💬 Communicate

How well did it work? Is the problem solved? Write a statement to describe how your model meets the guidelines of the task and why it is successful.

_____

_____

_____

🌟 Reflect

How did the buildings' roof features affect the temperature of their interiors? How would people who live in these types of buildings experience summer and winter?

_____

_____

_____

Name _____

Read the task. Then, follow the steps to complete the task.

It's in My Veins: The Human Body

Create a tube with "safety valves" that only allow a one-way flow of sand.

Materials

toilet paper roll cut in half
   lengthwise
scissors

small piece of heavy
   cardboard
tape
sand

Ask

What do you already know? What do you need to know to get started? Where can you find the information you need?

_____

_____

Imagine

What are the possibilities? Come up with several different options.

_____

_____

Plan

Choose an idea. Draw a model and label it. Consider making different models for each stage of construction or separate diagrams of more complex parts.

Plan

What are your steps? Use your drawing to guide your plan. Number your steps and write clearly so others can understand them.

_____

_____

_____

_____

Create

Follow your plan to create your model. What worked? What didn't? What did you need to change as you went through your plan? Why?

_____

_____

_____

Improve

How could you improve your model? Do you need to start over, or can you redo a single part? If it works, can it work even better?

_____

_____

_____

Communicate

How well did it work? Is the problem solved? Write a statement to describe how your model meets the guidelines of the task and why it is successful.

_____

_____

_____

Reflect

How did gravity affect the way sand moved through the tube? How do such valves work in human veins and the human heart?

_____

_____

_____

_____

Name _____

Read the task. Then, follow the steps to complete the task.

Keep Me in Suspense!

Create a suspension bridge that can hold a canned soft drink. Use the box sides as the ends to which you connect the bridge.

Materials

1 or 2 cardboard boxes   canned soft drink
string or yarn   narrow piece of
craft sticks   cardboard (optional)
tape

Ask

What do you already know? What do you need to know to get started? Where can you find the information you need?

_____

_____

_____

Imagine

What are the possibilities? Come up with several different options.

_____

_____

_____

Plan

Choose an idea. Draw a model and label it. Consider making different models for each stage of construction or separate diagrams of more complex parts.

Plan

What are your steps? Use your drawing to guide your plan. Number your steps and write clearly so others can understand them.

_____

_____

_____

Create

Follow your plan to create your model. What worked? What didn't? What did you need to change as you went through your plan? Why?

_____

_____

Improve

How could you improve your model? Do you need to start over, or can you redo a single part? If it works, can it work even better?

_____

_____

Communicate

How well did it work? Is the problem solved? Write a statement to describe how your model meets the guidelines of the task and why it is successful.

_____

_____

Reflect

How did your arrangement of the string or yarn help strengthen the bridge?

_____

_____

_____

Name _____

Read the task. Then, follow the steps to complete the task.

Going for a Ride: Simple Machines

Create a miniature catapult that will send a bead or ball of paper into a nearby bowl.

Materials

15 to 20 dominoes	clay
spoon	craft stick
bowl	tape
bead or ball of paper	

Ask

What do you already know? What do you need to know to get started? Where can you find the information you need?

_____

_____

_____

Imagine

What are the possibilities? Come up with several different options.

_____

_____

_____

Plan

Choose an idea. Draw a model and label it. Consider making different models for each stage of construction or separate diagrams of more complex parts.

📝 Plan

What are your steps? Use your drawing to guide your plan. Number your steps and write clearly so others can understand them.

_____

_____

_____

_____

✂️ Create

Follow your plan to create your model. What worked? What didn't? What did you need to change as you went through your plan? Why?

_____

_____

_____

🔄 Improve

How could you improve your model? Do you need to start over, or can you redo a single part? If it works, can it work even better?

_____

_____

_____

💬 Communicate

How well did it work? Is the problem solved? Write a statement to describe how your model meets the guidelines of the task and why it is successful.

_____

_____

_____

☀️ Reflect

How did your design of the catapult affect the speed and direction of the bead or ball of paper?

_____

_____

_____

_____

Name _____

Read the task. Then, follow the steps to complete the task.

Come On In!

Create a picket fence with a gate that can open and close.

Materials

craft sticks	paper clips
glue	pencils
clay	rubber bands

Ask

What do you already know? What do you need to know to get started? Where can you find the information you need?

_____

_____

_____

Imagine

What are the possibilities? Come up with several different options.

_____

_____

_____

Plan

Choose an idea. Draw a model and label it. Consider making different models for each stage of construction or separate diagrams of more complex parts.

📝 Plan

What are your steps? Use your drawing to guide your plan. Number your steps and write clearly so others can understand them.

_____

_____

_____

_____

🛠 Create

Follow your plan to create your model. What worked? What didn't? What did you need to change as you went through your plan? Why?

_____

_____

_____

🔄 Improve

How could you improve your model? Do you need to start over, or can you redo a single part? If it works, can it work even better?

_____

_____

_____

💬 Communicate

How well did it work? Is the problem solved? Write a statement to describe how your model meets the guidelines of the task and why it is successful.

_____

_____

_____

🔆 Reflect

How did your knowledge of door hinges help you?

_____

_____

_____

_____

Name _____

Read the task. Then, follow the steps to complete the task.

The Last Parachute

Create a parachute that takes the longest amount of time to reach the ground. Be sure to use identical weights and the same amount of string and tape when testing different designs.

Materials

scissors
a variety of materials, such as plastic bags, tissue paper, and fabric
string or yarn

tape
weights, such as coins or small plastic toys
stopwatch

Ask

What do you already know? What do you need to know to get started? Where can you find the information you need?

_____

_____

_____

Imagine

What are the possibilities? Come up with several different options.

_____

_____

_____

Plan

Choose an idea. Draw a model and label it. Consider making different models for each stage of construction or separate diagrams of more complex parts.

Plan

What are your steps? Use your drawing to guide your plan. Number your steps and write clearly so others can understand them.

_____

_____

_____

_____

Create

Follow your plan to create your model. What worked? What didn't? What did you need to change as you went through your plan? Why?

_____

_____

_____

Improve

How could you improve your model? Do you need to start over, or can you redo a single part? If it works, can it work even better?

_____

_____

_____

Communicate

How well did it work? Is the problem solved? Write a statement to describe how your model meets the guidelines of the task and why it is successful.

_____

_____

_____

Reflect

How did the materials you used affect the flight of the parachutes?

_____

_____

_____

_____

Name _____

Read the task. Then, follow the steps to complete the task.

Bobblehead Dolls

Create a bobblehead doll of your choice.

Materials

clay	toothpicks
egg carton segment	markers
paper clips	fabric (optional)
pencil	

Ask

What do you already know? What do you need to know to get started? Where can you find the information you need?

_____

_____

_____

Imagine

What are the possibilities? Come up with several different options.

_____

_____

_____

Plan

Choose an idea. Draw a model and label it. Consider making different models for each stage of construction or separate diagrams of more complex parts.

📓 Plan

What are your steps? Use your drawing to guide your plan. Number your steps and write clearly so others can understand them.

_____

_____

_____

_____

🛠 Create

Follow your plan to create your model. What worked? What didn't? What did you need to change as you went through your plan? Why?

_____

_____

_____

🔄 Improve

How could you improve your model? Do you need to start over, or can you redo a single part? If it works, can it work even better?

_____

_____

_____

💬 Communicate

How well did it work? Is the problem solved? Write a statement to describe how your model meets the guidelines of the task and why it is successful.

_____

_____

_____

☀ Reflect

How did the weight of the clay in the head affect how the bobbling worked?

_____

_____

_____

_____

 © Carson-Dellosa · CD-104856 · Applying the Standards: STEM

Name _____

Read the task. Then, follow the steps to complete the task.

"Weigh" to Go!

Create a ramp to test the speeds of a toy car when it carries different weights.

Materials

toy car	cardboard
weights, such as coins	books
tape	stopwatch

Ask

What do you already know? What do you need to know to get started? Where can you find the information you need?

_____

_____

_____

Imagine

What are the possibilities? Come up with several different options.

_____

_____

_____

Plan

Choose an idea. Draw a model and label it. Consider making different models for each stage of construction or separate diagrams of more complex parts.

📓 Plan

What are your steps? Use your drawing to guide your plan. Number your steps and write clearly so others can understand them.

_____

_____

_____

_____

🛠️ Create

Follow your plan to create your model. What worked? What didn't? What did you need to change as you went through your plan? Why?

_____

_____

_____

🔄 Improve

How could you improve your model? Do you need to start over, or can you redo a single part? If it works, can it work even better?

_____

_____

_____

💬 Communicate

How well did it work? Is the problem solved? Write a statement to describe how your model meets the guidelines of the task and why it is successful.

_____

_____

_____

☀️ Reflect

How did the weights you added to the toy car affect its speed?

_____

_____

_____

_____

Name _____

Read the task. Then, follow the steps to complete the task.

Test the Wind

Create a weather vane.

Materials

cardboard	tape
construction paper	compass
craft sticks	small toys
chenille stems	clay (optional)

 Ask

What do you already know? What do you need to know to get started? Where can you find the information you need?

_____

_____

_____

Imagine

What are the possibilities? Come up with several different options.

_____

_____

_____

Plan

Choose an idea. Draw a model and label it. Consider making different models for each stage of construction or separate diagrams of more complex parts.

📝 Plan

What are your steps? Use your drawing to guide your plan. Number your steps and write clearly so others can understand them.

_____

_____

_____

⚒ Create

Follow your plan to create your model. What worked? What didn't? What did you need to change as you went through your plan? Why?

_____

_____

_____

🔄 Improve

How could you improve your model? Do you need to start over, or can you redo a single part? If it works, can it work even better?

_____

_____

_____

💬 Communicate

How well did it work? Is the problem solved? Write a statement to describe how your model meets the guidelines of the task and why it is successful.

_____

_____

_____

☀ Reflect

How much wind was needed to turn your weather vane? What did you find when you used your compass to test wind direction?

_____

_____

_____

Name _____

Read the task. Then, follow the steps to complete the task.

Morse Phone?

Create a device through which you can send and receive a Morse code message.

Materials

2 paper cups   washer
pencil   metal spoon
string

A ·—	N —·
B —···	O ———
C —·—·	P ·——·
D —··	Q ——·—
E ·	R ·—·
F ··—·	S ···
G ——·	T —
H ····	U ··—
I ··	V ···—
J ·———	W ·——
K —·—	X —··—
L ·—··	Y —·——
M ——	Z ——··

Caution: Some methods of cutting holes in paper cups can cause injury if not done with care. This should only be done with the use of goggles and with adult supervision.

Ask

What do you already know? What do you need to know to get started? Where can you find the information you need?

_____

_____

_____

Imagine

What are the possibilities? Come up with several different options.

_____

_____

_____

Plan

Choose an idea. Draw a model and label it. Consider making different models for each stage of construction or separate diagrams of more complex parts.

📝 Plan

What are your steps? Use your drawing to guide your plan. Number your steps and write clearly so others can understand them.

_____

_____

_____

_____

🔧 Create

Follow your plan to create your model. What worked? What didn't? What did you need to change as you went through your plan? Why?

_____

_____

_____

🔄 Improve

How could you improve your model? Do you need to start over, or can you redo a single part? If it works, can it work even better?

_____

_____

_____

💬 Communicate

How well did it work? Is the problem solved? Write a statement to describe how your model meets the guidelines of the task and why it is successful.

_____

_____

_____

☀️ Reflect

How was the sound transfer of Morse code signals different from a voice through the phone?

_____

_____

_____

Name _____

Read the task. Then, follow the steps to complete the task.

Don't Lose Your Marbles!

Create a marble run that includes at least one tunnel, one jump, and one domino-related activity. Time the runs as you use different marbles.

Materials

several marbles	clay
toilet paper tubes	paintbrush
several books	tape
string	10 to 15 dominoes
cardboard	stopwatch
craft sticks	fabric (optional)
aluminum foil	

Ask

What do you already know? What do you need to know to get started? Where can you find the information you need?

_____

_____

_____

Imagine

What are the possibilities? Come up with several different options.

_____

_____

_____

Plan

Choose an idea. Draw a model and label it. Consider making different models for each stage of construction or separate diagrams of more complex parts.

📓 Plan

What are your steps? Use your drawing to guide your plan. Number your steps and write clearly so others can understand them.

_____

_____

_____

⚒️ Create

Follow your plan to create your model. What worked? What didn't? What did you need to change as you went through your plan? Why?

_____

_____

_____

🔄 Improve

How could you improve your model? Do you need to start over, or can you redo a single part? If it works, can it work even better?

_____

_____

_____

💬 Communicate

How well did it work? Is the problem solved? Write a statement to describe how your model meets the guidelines of the task and why it is successful.

_____

_____

_____

☀️ Reflect

How did your design affect the different marbles' times? What would you change about your run after seeing each marble go through?

_____

_____

_____

© Carson-Dellosa · CD-104856 · Applying the Standards: STEM

Name _____

Read the task. Then, follow the steps to complete the task.

Feed the Birds

Create a bird feeder.

Materials

pieces of wood
craft sticks
small boxes
a variety of containers,
    such as empty milk
    cartons and plastic
    bowls, cups, and plates

glue
a variety of decorating
    materials, such as
    markers and paint
birdseed

 Ask

What do you already know? What do you need to know to get started? Where can you find the information you need?

_____

_____

_____

Imagine

What are the possibilities? Come up with several different options.

_____

_____

_____

Plan

Choose an idea. Draw a model and label it. Consider making different models for each stage of construction or separate diagrams of more complex parts.

📝 Plan

What are your steps? Use your drawing to guide your plan. Number your steps and write clearly so others can understand them.

_____

_____

_____

_____

✂️ Create

Follow your plan to create your model. What worked? What didn't? What did you need to change as you went through your plan? Why?

_____

_____

_____

🔄 Improve

How could you improve your model? Do you need to start over, or can you redo a single part? If it works, can it work even better?

_____

_____

_____

💬 Communicate

How well did it work? Is the problem solved? Write a statement to describe how your model meets the guidelines of the task and why it is successful.

_____

_____

_____

☀️ Reflect

How does your bird feeder allow birds to obtain birdseed? What would you change about your bird feeder to keep out squirrels?

_____

_____

_____

_____

Name _____

Read the task. Then, follow the steps to complete the task.

Swinging: Force and Motion

Create a pendulum.

Materials

cardboard box	washer
craft sticks	tape
pencil	glue
string	stopwatch

Caution: Some methods of cutting holes in cardboard can cause injury if not done with care. This should only be done with the use of goggles and with adult supervision.

Ask

What do you already know? What do you need to know to get started? Where can you find the information you need?

_____

_____

_____

Imagine

What are the possibilities? Come up with several different options.

_____

_____

_____

Plan

Choose an idea. Draw a model and label it. Consider making different models for each stage of construction or separate diagrams of more complex parts.

▦ Plan

What are your steps? Use your drawing to guide your plan. Number your steps and write clearly so others can understand them.

_____

_____

_____

✂ Create

Follow your plan to create your model. What worked? What didn't? What did you need to change as you went through your plan? Why?

_____

_____

_____

↻ Improve

How could you improve your model? Do you need to start over, or can you redo a single part? If it works, can it work even better?

_____

_____

_____

◯ Communicate

How well did it work? Is the problem solved? Write a statement to describe how your model meets the guidelines of the task and why it is successful.

_____

_____

_____

☀ Reflect

How did creating a pendulum help you understand gravity and inertia?

_____

_____

_____

Name _____

Read the task. Then, follow the steps to complete the task.

Sailing the Seas

Create a sail that makes a sailboat travel fastest.

Materials

empty cardboard milk carton	fabric
clay	scissors
craft sticks	tabletop fan
string	large container filled with water
tape	stopwatch

 Ask

What do you already know? What do you need to know to get started? Where can you find the information you need?

_____

_____

_____

Imagine

What are the possibilities? Come up with several different options.

_____

_____

_____

Plan

Choose an idea. Draw a model and label it. Consider making different models for each stage of construction or separate diagrams of more complex parts.

📝 Plan

What are your steps? Use your drawing to guide your plan. Number your steps and write clearly so others can understand them.

_____

_____

_____

_____

🛠️ Create

Follow your plan to create your model. What worked? What didn't? What did you need to change as you went through your plan? Why?

_____

_____

_____

🔄 Improve

How could you improve your model? Do you need to start over, or can you redo a single part? If it works, can it work even better?

_____

_____

_____

💬 Communicate

How well did it work? Is the problem solved? Write a statement to describe how your model meets the guidelines of the task and why it is successful.

_____

_____

_____

☀️ Reflect

Why did the sail that made the sailboat travel fastest work the best? How did the shape of the other sails affect their speed?

_____

_____

_____

_____

Name _____

Read the task. Then, follow the steps to complete the task.

Move It: The Human Body

Create two models of human body joints—a ball-and-socket joint and a hinge joint. Move your knee and shoulder to compare them with the joints you create.

Materials

spherical lollipops	craft sticks
aluminum foil	glue
small cups	tape
cardboard	clay (optional)

Ask

What do you already know? What do you need to know to get started? Where can you find the information you need?

_____

_____

_____

Imagine

What are the possibilities? Come up with several different options.

_____

_____

_____

Plan

Choose an idea. Draw a model and label it. Consider making different models for each stage of construction or separate diagrams of more complex parts.

📓 Plan

What are your steps? Use your drawing to guide your plan. Number your steps and write clearly so others can understand them.

_____

_____

_____

_____

🛠️ Create

Follow your plan to create your model. What worked? What didn't? What did you need to change as you went through your plan? Why?

_____

_____

_____

🔄 Improve

How could you improve your model? Do you need to start over, or can you redo a single part? If it works, can it work even better?

_____

_____

_____

💬 Communicate

How well did it work? Is the problem solved? Write a statement to describe how your model meets the guidelines of the task and why it is successful.

_____

_____

_____

☀️ Reflect

How did observing the way your shoulder and knee joints move help you create your models?

_____

_____

_____

_____

Name _____

Read the task. Then, follow the steps to complete the task.

A Table for Two

Use the fewest amount of craft sticks needed to create a mini-table that can support a canned soft drink.

Materials

craft sticks   tape
glue   canned soft drink

Ask

What do you already know? What do you need to know to get started? Where can you find the information you need?

_____

_____

_____

Imagine

What are the possibilities? Come up with several different options.

_____

_____

_____

Plan

Choose an idea. Draw a model and label it. Consider making different models for each stage of construction or separate diagrams of more complex parts.

📝 Plan

What are your steps? Use your drawing to guide your plan. Number your steps and write clearly so others can understand them.

_____

_____

_____

_____

🛠️ Create

Follow your plan to create your model. What worked? What didn't? What did you need to change as you went through your plan? Why?

_____

_____

_____

🔄 Improve

How could you improve your model? Do you need to start over, or can you redo a single part? If it works, can it work even better?

_____

_____

_____

💬 Communicate

How well did it work? Is the problem solved? Write a statement to describe how your model meets the guidelines of the task and why it is successful.

_____

_____

_____

☀️ Reflect

What shapes helped you create a mini-table that was strong enough to hold the weight?

_____

_____

_____

_____

Name _____

Read the task. Then, follow the steps to complete the task.

Take the Stairs

Create a staircase with a landing on each floor. Your stairs may be straight, spiral, or any other configuration. Each step must be able to support a coin.

Materials

cardboard	glue
scissors	tape
craft sticks	coins
chenille stems	

Ask

What do you already know? What do you need to know to get started? Where can you find the information you need?

_____

_____

_____

Imagine

What are the possibilities? Come up with several different options.

_____

_____

_____

Plan

Choose an idea. Draw a model and label it. Consider making different models for each stage of construction or separate diagrams of more complex parts.

📝 Plan

What are your steps? Use your drawing to guide your plan. Number your steps and write clearly so others can understand them.

_____

_____

_____

_____

🛠 Create

Follow your plan to create your model. What worked? What didn't? What did you need to change as you went through your plan? Why?

_____

_____

_____

🔄 Improve

How could you improve your model? Do you need to start over, or can you redo a single part? If it works, can it work even better?

_____

_____

_____

💬 Communicate

How well did it work? Is the problem solved? Write a statement to describe how your model meets the guidelines of the task and why it is successful.

_____

_____

_____

☀ Reflect

How did your supporting structure help hold up your staircase?

_____

_____

_____

_____

Name _____

Read the task. Then, follow the steps to complete the task.

Like Oil and Water: Density

Create a device to test the density of different liquids.

Materials

clay	glue
paper cups	a variety of liquids, such
ruler or balsa wood	as cooking oil, water,
string	honey, and salt water
chenille stems	measuring cup (optional)

Caution: Before beginning any food activity, ask families' permission and inquire about students' food allergies and religious or other food restrictions.

Ask

What do you already know? What do you need to know to get started? Where can you find the information you need?

_____

_____

_____

Imagine

What are the possibilities? Come up with several different options.

_____

_____

_____

Plan

Choose an idea. Draw a model and label it. Consider making different models for each stage of construction or separate diagrams of more complex parts.

Plan

What are your steps? Use your drawing to guide your plan. Number your steps and write clearly so others can understand them.

_____

_____

_____

_____

Create

Follow your plan to create your model. What worked? What didn't? What did you need to change as you went through your plan? Why?

_____

_____

_____

Improve

How could you improve your model? Do you need to start over, or can you redo a single part? If it works, can it work even better?

_____

_____

_____

Communicate

How well did it work? Is the problem solved? Write a statement to describe how your model meets the guidelines of the task and why it is successful.

_____

_____

_____

Reflect

How did the amount of the liquids needed differ to get the device to equilibrium? What does that indicate about the densities of the liquids?

_____

_____

_____

_____

Name _____

Read the task. Then, follow the steps to complete the task.

Have a Seat!

Create a chair that can support a bottle of water.

Materials

a variety of dried pasta,
   such as angel hair, ziti,
   and elbow macaroni

glue
bottle of water

Ask

What do you already know? What do you need to know to get started? Where can you find the information you need?

_____

_____

_____

Imagine

What are the possibilities? Come up with several different options.

_____

_____

_____

Plan

Choose an idea. Draw a model and label it. Consider making different models for each stage of construction or separate diagrams of more complex parts.

📝 Plan

What are your steps? Use your drawing to guide your plan. Number your steps and write clearly so others can understand them.

_____

_____

_____

_____

🔧 Create

Follow your plan to create your model. What worked? What didn't? What did you need to change as you went through your plan? Why?

_____

_____

_____

🔄 Improve

How could you improve your model? Do you need to start over, or can you redo a single part? If it works, can it work even better?

_____

_____

_____

💬 Communicate

How well did it work? Is the problem solved? Write a statement to describe how your model meets the guidelines of the task and why it is successful.

_____

_____

_____

☀️ Reflect

How did the different types of pasta affect the strength of the chair?

_____

_____

_____

_____

Name _____

Read the task. Then, follow the steps to complete the task.

Get a Handle on It

Create a device that will allow you to lift a plastic spoon from the floor without directly touching the spoon.

Materials

paper clip	rubber bands
pencil	plates, bowls, and cups
cardboard	scissors
chenille stems	string or yarn
craft sticks	plastic spoon
clay	

Ask

What do you already know? What do you need to know to get started? Where can you find the information you need?

_____

_____

_____

Imagine

What are the possibilities? Come up with several different options.

_____

_____

_____

Plan

Choose an idea. Draw a model and label it. Consider making different models for each stage of construction or separate diagrams of more complex parts.

📝 Plan

What are your steps? Use your drawing to guide your plan. Number your steps and write clearly so others can understand them.

_____

_____

_____

✖️ Create

Follow your plan to create your model. What worked? What didn't? What did you need to change as you went through your plan? Why?

_____

_____

🔄 Improve

How could you improve your model? Do you need to start over, or can you redo a single part? If it works, can it work even better?

_____

_____

💬 Communicate

How well did it work? Is the problem solved? Write a statement to describe how your model meets the guidelines of the task and why it is successful.

_____

_____

☀️ Reflect

How did your device allow you to lift the spoon?

_____

_____

_____

Name _____

Read the task. Then, follow the steps to complete the task.

A Windy Day

Create a device that uses the wind to help sharpen a pencil.

Materials

paper cups	pencil
clay	string
cardboard	ruler
chenille stems	scissors
dowels	glue
craft sticks	tape
small pencil sharpener	tabletop fan
egg carton segment	

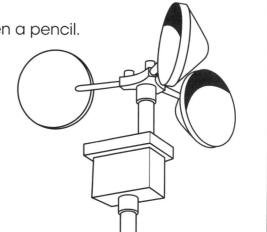

Ask

What do you already know? What do you need to know to get started? Where can you find the information you need?

_____

_____

_____

Imagine

What are the possibilities? Come up with several different options.

_____

_____

_____

Plan

Choose an idea. Draw a model and label it. Consider making different models for each stage of construction or separate diagrams of more complex parts.

Plan

What are your steps? Use your drawing to guide your plan. Number your steps and write clearly so others can understand them.

_____

_____

_____

_____

Create

Follow your plan to create your model. What worked? What didn't? What did you need to change as you went through your plan? Why?

_____

_____

_____

Improve

How could you improve your model? Do you need to start over, or can you redo a single part? If it works, can it work even better?

_____

_____

_____

Communicate

How well did it work? Is the problem solved? Write a statement to describe how your model meets the guidelines of the task and why it is successful.

_____

_____

_____

Reflect

How might energy from the wind be used to do other kinds of work?

_____

_____

_____

_____

Name _____

Read the task. Then, follow the steps to complete the task.

A Spider's Web

Create a spiderweb that is at least 1 foot (30 cm) in diameter that can withstand the force of a carefully tossed disposable foam ball.

Materials

string or thread

scissors

4 inches (10 cm) of tape

box

disposable foam ball

Ask

What do you already know? What do you need to know to get started? Where can you find the information you need?

_____

_____

_____

Imagine

What are the possibilities? Come up with several different options.

_____

_____

_____

Plan

Choose an idea. Draw a model and label it. Consider making different models for each stage of construction or separate diagrams of more complex parts.

✏️ Plan

What are your steps? Use your drawing to guide your plan. Number your steps and write clearly so others can understand them.

_____

_____

_____

🛠️ Create

Follow your plan to create your model. What worked? What didn't? What did you need to change as you went through your plan? Why?

_____

_____

🔄 Improve

How could you improve your model? Do you need to start over, or can you redo a single part? If it works, can it work even better?

_____

_____

💬 Communicate

How well did it work? Is the problem solved? Write a statement to describe how your model meets the guidelines of the task and why it is successful.

_____

_____

☀️ Reflect

How did your connections between the web material and the box help the web withstand the force of the ball?

_____

_____

_____

Name _____

Read the task. Then, follow the steps to complete the task.

Take a Ride!

Create a mini Ferris wheel that can move like the real thing.

Materials

cardboard	toothpicks
construction paper	paper clips
clay	dowel
craft sticks	scissors
chenille stems	glue
straws	tape

Ask

What do you already know? What do you need to know to get started? Where can you find the information you need?

_____

_____

_____

Imagine

What are the possibilities? Come up with several different options.

_____

_____

_____

Plan

Choose an idea. Draw a model and label it. Consider making different models for each stage of construction or separate diagrams of more complex parts.

📓 Plan

What are your steps? Use your drawing to guide your plan. Number your steps and write clearly so others can understand them.

_____

_____

_____

_____

🛠️ Create

Follow your plan to create your model. What worked? What didn't? What did you need to change as you went through your plan? Why?

_____

_____

_____

🔄 Improve

How could you improve your model? Do you need to start over, or can you redo a single part? If it works, can it work even better?

_____

_____

_____

💬 Communicate

How well did it work? Is the problem solved? Write a statement to describe how your model meets the guidelines of the task and why it is successful.

_____

_____

_____

☀️ Reflect

How did you support the outer ring of the wheel where the seats would be located?

_____

_____

_____

_____